THE YEAR OF
FAITH

A BIBLE STUDY GUIDE FOR CATHOLICS

FR. MITCH PACWA, S.J.

Our Sunday Visitor Publishing Division
Our Sunday Visitor, Inc.
Huntington, Indiana 46750

Nihil Obstat
Msgr. Michael Heintz, Ph.D.
Censor Librorum

Imprimatur
✠ Kevin C. Rhoades
Bishop of Fort Wayne-South Bend
May 25, 2012

The *Nihil Obstat* and *Imprimatur* are official declarations that a book is free from doctrinal or moral error. It is not implied that those who have granted the *Nihil Obstat* and *Imprimatur* agree with the contents, opinions, or statements expressed.

ISBN: 978-1-61278-623-0 (Inventory No. T1320)
eISBN: 978-1-61278-225-6
LCCN: 2012935983

Cover design: Lindsey Riesen
Cover art: The Crosiers
Interior design: Sherri L. Hoffman
Interior art: iStockPhoto.com

Printed in the United States of America

To my friend and classmate in the Society of Jesus,
Father J. Michael Sparough, S.J.

CONTENTS

FOREWORD

Father Mitch Pacwa, S.J., is a theologian well known for his ability to explain and interpret the Catholic faith to audiences familiar with his appearances on the Eternal Word Television Network. He enjoys a renown that requires no other endorsement than his words themselves.

In this book, we find another expression of Father Pacwa's ability to teach in a way that draws others ever more deeply into the mysteries of the faith. Pope Benedict XVI's proclaiming a Year of Faith is the occasion for the publication of this text that brings together Scripture and theology, using the method exemplified in the preaching and writing of the Holy Father himself.

Faith gives theology its subject matter or data from God's self-revelation in human history. Faith tells us that the books of Scripture that proclaim the mighty works of God are the word of God in human words. Since faith and reason are partners in the human pursuit of truth, the believer is impelled by faith to explore the sacred texts of Scripture and reflect upon them intelligently. Father Pacwa gives us a method for doing so, with well-chosen quotes from the Bible and the Magisterium. His own words are a solid guide that offers commentary designed to inform our mind and stir our heart.

In this book, we find what Pope Benedict has said in his own words after the 2008 Synod on the Word of God in the Life and Mission of the Church: " . . . the interpretation of sacred Scripture presupposes the harmony of faith and reason. On the one hand, it calls for a faith which, by maintaining a proper relationship with right reason, never degenerates into fideism, which in the case of Scripture would end up in fundamentalism. On the other hand, it calls for a reason which, in its investigation of the historical elements present in the Bible, is marked by openness and does not reject *a priori* anything beyond its own terms of reference" (*Verbum Domini*, n. 36).

Pope Benedict often insists that faith begins with a relationship. Only because one has a living relationship with God in Jesus Christ through the power of the Holy Spirit does one desire to know more deeply who Christ is and live more authentically as his disciple. Knowing who Christ is gives birth to doctrine, and living as his disciple requires moral teaching. But without a relationship to Christ, doctrine is just ideas and morality is only rules. Relationships give life. Relationship to Christ leads us to introduce others to him and increase the circle of his friends gathered into his body, the Church. This book is a handbook for mission, a tool for deepening our relationship to Christ and for introducing others to him. It can be used alone or for group Bible study.

The Second Vatican Council, whose fiftieth anniversary the Church celebrates with this Year of Faith, was a missionary council called to help the Church change her relationship to the world so that the entire world would unite around its Savior. Fifty years after the council, the world is more united in global communications systems, in its financial order, and in ecological consciousness; but this global unity risks basing itself on a false claim to autonomy and to fake independence. Only a living relationship established through dialogue with God will prevent the world from becoming ever more closed in on itself. Without this relationship to God, we live in a prison of our own making.

Father Pacwa's book presents a formula for breaking out of self-imposed prisons. Scripture read in the community of faith opens our lives to a greater world called the kingdom of God. This kingdom is not a place but a person: Jesus. Through prayer and the study of Scripture we are given insight into the beginnings of the world and told about its end. In Scripture, we find out who we are and what is our destiny. In Scripture, we discover explicitly what our hearts already know intuitively: Jesus is "the first and the last" (Rev 1:17).

Using this book should bring light to our minds and joy to our hearts. I am grateful for a well-conceived work that bears witness to Father Pacwa's own life of faith. If the Church is to be a leaven working in the world to open it to its Creator, then everyone's faith must be deepened and made more vital. This is a book for everyone.

✠ Francis Cardinal George, O.M.I.
Archbishop of Chicago

HOW TO USE THIS STUDY GUIDE IN A GROUP

This is an interactive study guide. It can be read with profit either alone or as part of a group Bible study. Below are suggestions for the use of this book in a group.

WHAT YOU WILL NEED FOR EVERY SESSION

- This study guide
- A Bible
- A notebook

- **Before Session 1, members of the group are encouraged to read the Introduction and Session 1 and to complete all of the exercises in both.** They should bring this study guide with them to the group session.
- **Begin the session with prayer** (for example, An Act of Faith, on page 93).
- **Invite one person in the group to read one of the Scripture passages included in this session's material.**
- **Allow five minutes of silent reflection on the passage.** This allows the group to quiet their inner thoughts and to center themselves on the lesson to be discussed.
- **Catechesis:** Give all members a chance to share some point that they have learned about the Year of Faith. Was this something new or a new insight into something? Was there anything that raised a question? (Allow fifteen to twenty minutes for this.)

- **Discussion:** Use the discussion questions at the end of the session chapter to begin a deeper grasp of the material covered in the session. (Allow fifteen to twenty minutes for this.)
- **Conclusion:** Have all members of the group summarize the key concepts they learned about the Year of Faith discussed in the session. Assign the next session as homework, to be completed before the next group session.

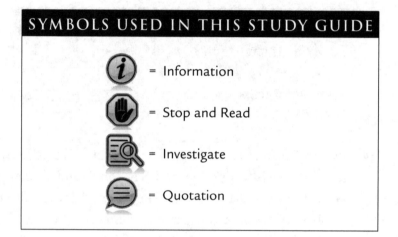

SYMBOLS USED IN THIS STUDY GUIDE

= Information

= Stop and Read

= Investigate

= Quotation

ACKNOWLEDGMENTS

The Scripture citations used in this work are taken from the *Second Catholic Edition of the Revised Standard Version of the Bible* (RSV), copyright © 1965, 1966, and 2006 by the Division of Christian Education of the National Council of the Churches of Christ in the United States of America. Used by permission. All rights reserved.

The English translation of the *Catechism of the Catholic Church* for the United States of America is copyrighted, © 1994, United States Catholic Conference, Inc. — Libreria Editrice Vaticana. The English translation of the *Catechism of the Catholic Church: Modifications from the Editio Typica* is copyrighted, © 1997, United States Catholic Conference, Inc. — Libreria Editrice Vaticana.

Quotations from the apostolic letter *Porta Fidei* and other papal statements are copyrighted, © 2012, Libreria Editrice Vaticana.

The English translation of the Nicene Creed is by the International Consultation on English Texts (ICET).

Excerpts from the English translation of *The Roman Missal* © 2010, International Commission on English in the Liturgy Corporation (ICEL); excerpt from the English translation of the *Rite of Baptism for Children* © 1969, ICEL. All rights reserved.

Introduction

A YEAR OF FAITH

> "Ever since the start of my ministry as Successor of Peter, I have spoken of the need to rediscover the journey of faith so as to shed ever clearer light on the joy and renewed enthusiasm of the encounter with Christ. During the homily at the Mass marking the inauguration of my pontificate I said: "The Church as a whole and all her Pastors, like Christ, must set out to lead people out of the desert, towards the place of life, towards friendship with the Son of God, towards the One who gives us life, and life in abundance."
> — Pope Benedict XVI,
> *Porta Fidei* (n. 2)

In his apostolic letter *Porta Fidei* (October 11, 2011), Pope Benedict XVI announced a Year of Faith to begin on October 11, 2012, and end on November 24, 2013. As part of this special year, he calls on all Catholics to renew their faith in the Father, the Son, and the Holy Spirit, in the teachings of Christ and in the doctrines of the Church.

The Year of Faith will celebrate three occasions:

- The *first* occasion, the start of the Year of Faith on October 11, will mark the fiftieth anniversary of the opening of the Second Vatican Council on October 11, 1962. One goal of this year will be to have the council documents "read correctly," to make them "widely known," and to see them as "normative texts" of the Church's Magisterium (n. 5).

- The *second* occasion is the twentieth anniversary of the publication of the *Catechism of the Catholic Church* on October 11, 1992. The Year of Faith will orient Catholics to "rediscover and study the fundamental content of the faith," and to recognize that the *Catechism* is the "indispensable tool" to synthesize it (n. 11).

- The *third* occasion is the Synod on New Evangelization, which will take place in October 2012. The pope wants the Year of Faith to help Christians "radiate the word of truth" (n. 6) because the "love of Christ . . . impels us to evangelize" (n. 7). "Faith grows," he says, "when it is lived as an experience of love received and when it is communicated as an experience of grace and joy" (n. 7).

CONSIDER

In *Porta Fidei*, Pope Benedict invites us to walk through the perpetually open "door of faith" (n. 1; Acts 14:27) as a way of finding direction for our life's journey. From the moment of conception, every person is on a journey that moves through life, death, and beyond. For many people, the journey has an unknown goal, and their life appears aimless. Some move from one temporary stop to another, as if going from oasis to oasis, for some pleasures and rest wherever they can find them. Others see only a desert stretching out to the horizon, whose shifting sands cover any tracks or pathways. These travelers do not know which direction to take in life, nor do they know where they are headed.

Pope Benedict quotes his inaugural sermon as pope to describe how Christ and the Church must "lead people out of the desert, towards the place of life, towards friendship with the Son of God, towards the One who gives us life, and life in abundance"

(n. 2). Throughout *Porta Fidei*, Benedict describes the journey of faith and its many components. We will study these aspects of the journey in this book.

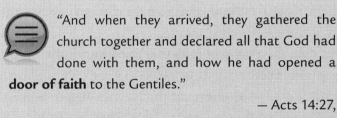

"And when they arrived, they gathered the church together and declared all that God had done with them, and how he had opened a **door of faith** to the Gentiles."

— Acts 14:27, emphasis added

STUDY

The *Catechism* and the Documents of Vatican II
As part of your celebration of the Year of Faith, I suggest that you make time for reading important documents on the Catholic faith.

First, I urge you to make it a goal to read the *Catechism of the Catholic Church*. It is the official systematic presentation of Catholic doctrine. The *Catechism* is structured on four themes: "The Profession of Faith" (centering on the Creed), "The Celebration of the Christian Mystery" (focusing on the sacraments), "Life in Christ" (emphasizing the Beatitudes and the Ten Commandments), and "Christian Prayer" (focusing especially on prayer traditions and the Our Father). (Before tackling the *Catechism* itself, you may want to read one of the shorter versions: the *Compendium of the Catechism of the Catholic Church* or the *United States Catholic Catechism for Adults*.)

Second, I suggest that you read two important documents of the Second Vatican Council: *Lumen Gentium* (Dogmatic Constitution on the Church) and *Dei Verbum* (Dogmatic Constitution on Divine Revelation). The council designed these documents to shape our lives as Catholics, and as such they deserve our careful and prayerful study.

Notice how frequently each of these documents quotes Sacred Scripture. As you read the documents, look up these passages, bring them to prayer, and consider the links between the Bible passages and the council teachings.

Try to gain the vision of faith and the Church that these documents contain. Then bring this vision to your own understanding of the faith and to your efforts at the New Evangelization.

New Evangelization means calling everyone to have faith in God as he is revealed by Jesus Christ. It is a re-commitment to a personal love of Christ in union with the Church. It is a discovery of life and grace in the sacraments and a recovery of receiving the Bible as the Word of God.

CONSIDER

Pope Benedict recognizes, in *Porta Fidei*, the "profound crisis of faith that has affected many people" (n. 2). He identifies "grave difficulties of the time, especially with regard to the profession of the true faith and its correct interpretation" (n. 5). The pope says that several contemporary tendencies erode faith.

First, much of the modern mentality "limits the field of rational certainties to that of scientific and technological discoveries" (n. 12). Many hold that if science cannot prove something the Church teaches and people believe, that belief is regarded merely as a matter of personal feelings.

Second, the pope notes that a certain portion of the cultural elites — especially in the universities and much of the media — denies the existence of God and denounces the role of the Church. For example, "New Atheists" like Richard Dawkins and Sam Harris present few coherent arguments for the non-existence of God. Rather, they spew vitriol against God and ridicule those who believe in him. (And yet, in February 2012, Dawkins himself admitted that he can't be certain that God doesn't exist, and that he would call himself an agnostic rather than an atheist.)

Third, Benedict observes that the vast majority of Americans who express belief in God — about 90 percent — put God and faith into one compartment of their life. They isolate him from their social life, morality, and regular use of personal time. God might get a smile and a tip of the hat, but he is not the center, the goal, or the meaning of life for many of those who profess belief in him.

> "Dear brothers and sisters, this is true for every Christian: faith is first and foremost a personal, intimate encounter with Jesus, it is having an experience of his closeness, his friendship and his love. It is in this way that we learn to know him ever better, to love him and to follow him more and more. May this happen to each one of us!"
> — Pope Benedict XVI,
> General Audience (October 21, 2009)

For these reasons, Pope Benedict has called for a Year of Faith. He wants all Christians who already believe to ask the Lord to help their unbelief (see Mk 9:24). The goal of the year will be a conversion by which believers turn to follow Jesus Christ more closely. Conversion means an acceptance of those things God wants to communicate about himself, about being the humans he created us to be, and about salvation.

We can use human reason to discover some of these truths. For example, reason can tell us that a marvelously intelligent and powerful being created the universe and established the principles that govern it. But faith builds on reason and completes the picture. It leads to the realization that since God is greater than everything in the universe, he deserves to be loved above all things. Faith draws us to make God our singular purpose and to place him at the center of our hearts. Knowing and loving him gives us meaning. He integrates every component of our life — relationships, morality, work, recreation, and all — into a meaningful whole.

Growing in a faith that allows a loving God to become our purpose is a gradual process. But we can make much progress during this year by responding to Pope Benedict's call and teaching: "May this Year of Faith make our relationship with Christ the Lord increasingly firm, since only in him is there the certitude for looking to the future and the guarantee of an authentic and lasting love" (*Porta Fidei*, n. 15).

Session 1

BELIEF IN JESUS CHRIST

"We must rediscover a taste for feeding ourselves on the word of God, faithfully handed down by the Church, and on the bread of life, offered as sustenance for his disciples (cf. Jn 6:51). Indeed, the teaching of Jesus still resounds in our day with the same power: 'Do not labor for the food which perishes, but for the food which endures to eternal life' (Jn 6:27). The question posed by his listeners is the same that we ask today: 'What must we do, to be doing the works of God?' (Jn 6:28). We know Jesus' reply: 'This is the work of God, that you believe in him whom he has sent' (Jn 6:29). Belief in Jesus Christ, then, is the way to arrive definitively at salvation."

— Pope Benedict XVI,
Porta Fidei (n. 3)

In this Year of Faith, exactly what do we have faith in?

The answer is not what, but whom. As Pope Benedict says, "During this time we will need to keep our gaze fixed upon Jesus Christ, the 'pioneer and perfecter of our faith' (Heb 12:2)" (*Porta Fidei*, n. 13).

Jesus began his ministry with the announcement, known in Greek as the *kerygma*, "The time is fulfilled, and the kingdom of God is at hand; repent, and believe in the gospel" (Mk 1:15). Notice here the sequence of phrases: the summons to faith is the result of repentance. This means that turning away from sin prepares the heart to be open to faith. Jesus first commands repentance — the examination of the conscience regarding offences against God and other humans — followed by a rejection of these sinful choices.

Next, Jesus summons everyone to "believe in the gospel." At this early moment of Jesus' public ministry, the Gospel consists of the simple announcement that "the time is fulfilled, and the kingdom of God is at hand." But these simple phrases provoke important questions. Why is the time fulfilled now? How is the kingdom of God at hand? One is meant to read the rest of the Gospel with such questions as the backdrop.

The central key to answering these questions is that the fulfillment of time and the presence of the kingdom depend on the presence of Jesus Christ himself. St. Matthew's Gospel in particular (and the others as well) highlights passages from the Old Testament, which Jesus fulfills from his birth through his resurrection.

THE FULFILLMENT OF THE OLD TESTAMENT PROPHECIES

Matthew's Gospel was written for a community of Jewish Christians. They were quite familiar with the Old Testament, so it was extra important for Matthew to frequently point out the Old Testament prophecies that Jesus fulfilled. Mark and Luke were written for largely Gentile communities that did not have the same familiarity with the Old Testament. Interestingly, in Luke 24, Jesus twice is described as explaining the ways he fulfills the Old Testament. Then, in the Acts of the Apostles, also written by St. Luke, Old Testament texts are often quoted, particularly as the apostles and disciples preach to Jewish people.

INVESTIGATE

PROPHECIES FULFILLED

Look up some of the Old Testament prophecies that Jesus fulfills in Matthew's Gospel. Skim through the Gospel looking for the phrase, "This was to fulfill. . . ." Look at the bottom of the page of your Bible and find the verse number you have chosen. There you will see references to the Old Testament verse being cited. For example, the first occurrence of "fulfill" occurs in Matthew 1:22-23. Look for the reference to verse 23 and you will see Isaiah 7:14 listed. Try this on your own with Matthew 2:15 and 8:17.

CONSIDER

Jesus uses various ways to bring the kingdom of God at hand. One way he demonstrates the power of the kingdom is by casting out demons. These acts show that the kingdom of darkness and the evil one are losing power to the kingdom of God precisely because Jesus is present to expel demons by his authoritative word.

Another sign of the presence of the kingdom of God is found in Jesus' healings and raising of the dead. These fulfill Old Testament promises that the lame will walk, the blind will see, and the deaf will hear. The healings also demonstrate the power of the kingdom of God to heal and transform people's lives. A key to understanding their importance is to note that the healings occur because of the authority of Jesus himself, which again points to Jesus as the content of the Gospel. Furthermore, Jesus evokes faith from the people he heals.

Yet another element to examine is the command to believe the Gospel. The content of the Gospel goes beyond the announcement of the fulfillment of time and the nearness of the kingdom of God. Jesus taught many things, and the people were "astonished at his teaching, for he taught them as one who had authority, and not as the scribes" (Mk 1:22).

INVESTIGATE

EXORCISMS

 Read the passages in Mark (1:21-27; 5:1-19; 9:14-29) that recount exorcisms by Jesus. Pay attention to the reactions of the demons themselves. Note also the reaction of faith by the people.

In Mark 1:21-27, how do the people in the synagogue react?

_____

_____

_____

In Mark 5:1-19, what is the reaction of the man from whom the legion of demons is cast out? What does the Gentile crowd from the "country of the Gerasenes" do?

_____

_____

_____

In Mark 9:14-29, what is Jesus' reaction to the father's lack of faith?

_____

_____

_____

How do you react to Jesus' power over the demonic forces?

_____

_____

_____

The rabbinic literature exists in collections of sayings by various leading rabbis. Their authority is cited and the learning process derives from reconciling the various teachers. Jesus is different from them because he never cites a rabbi as an authority to support his teaching; he is his own authority.

CONSIDER

One of the most astonishing and, to the non-believer, disturbing elements of the Gospels is Jesus' repeated demand to make an act of faith in the person of Jesus himself. Moses, Buddha, and Mohammed never made such requests for faith in their own person; rather, they focused on the message they brought. Distinctively, Jesus Christ claims to be the object of human faith.

The Christian does not only believe the ideas and moral teachings of Christ, nor is it enough for believers to recognize that he is a great prophet or miracle worker, though all of this is true. The Christian makes an act of faith in the person of Jesus Christ that draws the believer into a personal relationship with Jesus, characterized by love and trust. The believer trusts Jesus and loves him, even when things do not go well — disappointments, difficulties, challenges, rejection, and even persecution do not sever the relationship with Christ. They are events that must be confronted with the help, grace, and example of Jesus Christ, who suffered the same things and even worse ones.

One of the most amazing aspects of faith in Jesus is that it encompasses the horrible suffering and death he endured. Strangely, it was not an embarrassment for the early Christians that their Savior died like a slave and criminal on a cross, and they did not cover it up. Instead, his death on the cross became a central theme of the faith they spread throughout the ancient world.

Finally, faith in Jesus Christ also requires faith in his resurrection. Acceptance of this article of faith did not come easily to the disciples and apostles. The holy women went to Jesus' tomb on the first Easter to anoint a corpse, not to greet the resurrected Lord. Even as Mary Magdalene spoke to the risen Jesus, she did not consider that it might be her Lord but assumed he was the gardener (Jn 20:15). Only when he spoke her name did she recognize him (Jn 20:16). When the apostles saw the risen Jesus, some of them doubted that it was the Lord (Mt 28:17). All of the Resurrection narratives can be read as stories of conversion to faith in Jesus' resurrection.

INVESTIGATE

CONVERSION AND THE RESURRECTION

 Read Matthew 28, Mark 16, Luke 24, and John 20-21. Identify each occasion of conversion in the Resurrection of Jesus. Who converts? What convinces them?

_____

_____

_____

STUDY

Faith in Jesus' resurrection is essential to being a Christian, as St. Paul explicitly states. St. Paul tells us that a lack of faith in the Resurrection makes our faith vain and turns us into the most foolish of people. Without Christ's resurrection as a key doctrine of our faith, our sins are not forgiven. This means that it is not only the sacrificial death of Jesus on the cross that reconciles us to God but also his resurrection from the dead.

Stop here and read **1 Corinthians 15:12-28** in your own Bible.

In fact, the Resurrection grounds, in the facts of history, the Christian hope of future resurrection for every human being who ever lived or will live. As a result, life is full of meaning because God wants all of the redeemed to live forever. Because Christians have hope in their future resurrection, many of them over the centuries have given up self-satisfaction in order to serve God and other people. They have impoverished themselves in order to help the poor, the sick, and the needy. In fact, many millions have even undergone martyrdom and suffering for their faith in Jesus because they trust that their resurrection will make the present suffering worthwhile, just as it did for Jesus in his passion and death.

THE CENTRALITY OF THE CROSS

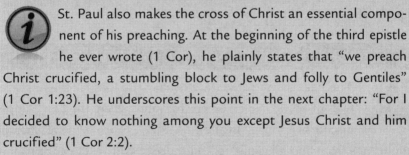 St. Paul also makes the cross of Christ an essential component of his preaching. At the beginning of the third epistle he ever wrote (1 Cor), he plainly states that "we preach Christ crucified, a stumbling block to Jews and folly to Gentiles" (1 Cor 1:23). He underscores this point in the next chapter: "For I decided to know nothing among you except Jesus Christ and him crucified" (1 Cor 2:2).

At the end of his epistle to the Galatians, the apostle undergirds all of his arguments by writing: "But far be it from me to glory except in the cross of our Lord Jesus Christ, by which the world has been crucified to me, and I to the world" (Gal 6:14).

When St. Paul gives his teaching on the reason that Baptism is powerful for the Christian, he grounds the sacrament in the cross and the resurrection (Rom 6:1-8), and he makes a similar point when

continued on next page…

he teaches about the meaning and power of the Eucharist: "For as often as you eat this bread and drink the cup, you proclaim the Lord's death until he comes" (1 Cor 11:26).

Then, in a hymn about Christ and his nature and mission, St. Paul writes:

> [Christ] who, though he was in the form of God, did not count equality with God a thing to be grasped, but emptied himself, taking the form of a servant, being born in the likeness of men. And being found in human form he humbled himself and became obedient unto death, even death on a cross. (Phil 2:6-8)

These and other professions of faith in the centrality of the cross of Jesus by St. Paul are all the more striking because he had persecuted the Christians who had preached the same thing before his conversion.

INVESTIGATE

THE PASSION: CENTRAL TO THE FAITH

The Passion narratives are usually the longest single narratives of each Gospel, except for John, where the Last Supper discourse is longer. In addition, the Passion narratives include quotations from and allusions to a number of Old Testament prophecies. This shows that the early Christians understood the events of Christ's passion as the fulfillment of prophecy and therefore part of God's long-planned way of preparing for the redemption of the world. Therefore, the Christian makes the passion and death of Jesus central to faith in him as the promised Messiah.

Connect the Old Testament prophecies with the Passion narratives in the Gospels:

- Daniel 7:13 with Matthew 26:64
- Zechariah 11:12-13 and Jeremiah 32:6-15; 18:2-3 with Matthew 27:9
- Psalm 22:7-8 with Mark 15:31
- Psalm 31:5 with Luke 23:46
- Job 1:6-12 and Amos 9:9 with Luke 22:31-32
- Isaiah 53:12 with Luke 22:37

Faith in the risen Lord Jesus offers hope and sets out a whole new task for the lives of the disciples. Faith is the summons that Jesus makes from the start of his public ministry all the way through to his ascension. Faith highlights and illumines the central themes of the Gospel. Let us allow faith to renew our reading and meditating on the Gospels in such a way that God's grace transforms our lives through it. As Pope Benedict tells us for this Year of Faith, "By faith, we too live: by the living recognition of the Lord Jesus, present in our lives and in our history" (*Porta Fidei*, n. 13).

DISCUSS

1. Who do you think Jesus is?
2. What difference does belief in Jesus make in your life?
3. What new insights have you gained from the Scripture passages you read in this chapter?

PRACTICE

This week make a conscious act of faith in Jesus and in his saving work in your life. Ask him to help increase your faith where it is weak.

Session 2

ASSENT TO THE CREED

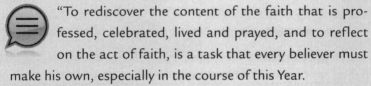"To rediscover the content of the faith that is professed, celebrated, lived and prayed, and to reflect on the act of faith, is a task that every believer must make his own, especially in the course of this Year.

"Not without reason, Christians in the early centuries were required to learn the creed from memory. It served them as a daily prayer not to forget the commitment they had undertaken in baptism. With words rich in meaning, Saint Augustine speaks of this in a homily on the *redditio symboli*, the handing over of the creed: 'the symbol of the holy mystery that you have all received together and that today you have recited one by one, are the words on which the faith of Mother Church is firmly built above the stable foundation that is Christ the Lord. You have received it and recited it, but in your minds and hearts you must keep it ever present, you must repeat it in your beds, recall it in the public squares and not forget it during meals: even when your body is asleep, you must watch over it with your hearts.' "

— Pope Benedict XVI,
Porta Fidei (n. 9)

Before we can make a true act of faith, we need to know and understand what exactly we believe to be true. The Creed outlines what we as Christians hold as the essential matters of truth from the earliest times. By examining how our articles of faith are directly and intrinsically linked to the teachings of Scripture, we can assent to the teachings of the Creed with our whole being, as Pope Benedict encourages us.

PERSECUTION SPREAD THE CHURCH

Despite the persecutions of the Jerusalem church by the Jewish authorities, and then persecutions by the Roman government, first in Rome and then around the empire for three centuries, followed by the persecution of Christians by various powers in other parts of the world, the Christian Church grew and spread widely. Many people of quite varied nationalities considered themselves Christian because they followed Jesus Christ and his teachings. That is essentially what the name Christian means — one who follows Jesus.

CONSIDER

Concern for the truth was always integral to the message of Jesus Christ. One area where Jesus was especially strong was in his rejection of the teachings of the Pharisees. In Mark 7:1-23 and Matthew 15:1-20, he criticized the Pharisees' focus on whether his disciples followed the mandates of the Pharisee tradition about washing hands before eating. He rebuked them for external observance of the tradition while they neglected the deeper truths of God. Another time, while in Jerusalem, Jesus gave a long critique of the Pharisees (Mt 23:1-35). Though he recognized their authority, he rejected them for failing to practice what they preached. Jesus did not tolerate any teaching or ethical practice that contradicted his own Gospel.

Not only did Jesus criticize false teaching and morals, but so did the Church after Pentecost. From the earliest years of the Church, as evidenced by many New Testament passages, some Christians began to change the content of the faith and morals that had been passed on to them by the apostles. Sts. Paul, James, Peter, John, and Jude wrote vigorous reproofs of those who taught falsely, and they corrected the teachings. They understood that the very core of the faith was at stake in their disputes with false teachers, and they addressed the issues strongly and publicly. Now their answers remain part of our Sacred Scriptures.

INVESTIGATE

HERESIES

Look up the following passages that deal with false teachings and heretical groups in the early Church. What were the errors contained in each variant form of Christianity? Some of the texts indicate the motives of those who taught error. Write down notes about those motives for falsehood.

PASSAGE	NOTES
Galatians 1:6-9; 2:4-5	
2 Corinthians 11:1-6, 12-15	
Philippians 3:2-11, 17-21	
1 Timothy 1:3-7, 18-20	
Hebrews 6:1-6	
2 Peter 2:1-3:4	
1 John 2:18-25; 4:1-6	

STUDY

The leaders of the early Church strongly and clearly rejected the various false doctrines that arose from among Christian believers and excluded those who taught falsehood from the Church. The early Church considered true and correct doctrine an important component of authentic faith in Jesus Christ. In countering false teachings, the true teachings were clarified and refined.

In the second century, Gnosticism arose as a catch-all term for people who considered themselves to be spiritually advanced. (*Gnosis* is the Greek work for knowledge.) They claimed to be so developed that they had direct spiritual knowledge of divine realities, thereby making them spiritual men and women. The Gnostics claimed to be free of the body and above the material world. They believed that the god who created the material world was the wicked deity of the Old Testament, while God the Father created the spiritual world. Gnostics also rejected the apostolic tradition and the New Testament as worldly teachings meant for the simple and unenlightened Christians who lived on faith.

Among the false teachings about God included the idea that the Father, the Son, and the Holy Spirit are not three Persons but three modes of the one divine Person as he relates to humans and the world. Another doctrine called Arianism held that Jesus Christ is not divine but was a creature made by the Father and was capable of sin.

Over the following centuries, other notions arose, such as Monophysitism, which taught that Jesus had only one divine nature, without a human soul that would make him truly human, and conversely, Nestorianism, which taught that there were two separate persons in Jesus, one divine and one human.

Fathers of the Church such as St. Irenaeus, St. Athanasius, and St. John Chrysostom opposed the heretics and wrote treatises that refuted their errors. And to preserve the orthodoxy of the faith, the bishops met in synods and councils to confront the false doctrines. These councils published decrees condemning the false teachings and issued clear statements of the Catholic faith in decrees and creeds, plus clarifying moral issues and Church discipline.

- 325 — **Nicaea** condemned Arianism and formulated the Nicene Creed.
- 381 — **I Constantinople** further condemned Arianism and added doctrines on the Holy Spirit to the Nicene Creed, making the present form the Nicene-Constantinopolitan Creed.
- 431 — **Ephesus** condemned Nestorianism and proclaimed Mary *Theotokos* ("God-bearer"), the Mother of God.
- 451 — **Chalcedon** condemned Monophysitism and taught the hypostatic union of the two natures of Christ.
- 553 — **II Constantinople** condemned Nestorianism.
- 680-681 — **III Constantinople** condemned Monothelitism, the teaching that Jesus did not have a human will in addition to his divine will.
- 787 — **II Nicaea** condemned Iconoclasm and permitted the veneration of icons.

CONSIDER

What is at stake when the Church defines doctrines in the councils and creeds? What were the councils trying to accomplish? On the one hand, the chief goal was maintaining the purity of the faith. The councils wanted to know whether a theologian's doctrine conformed to the faith passed on by the apostles to the bishops, or if it was an innovation that dismantled key doctrines and the integrity of the faith. On the other hand, the definitions of the faith were meant to maintain the balances that underlie each mystery of the faith.

STUDY

St. Paul mentions the term "mystery" in three of his epistles to describe the faith. At the same time, these passages announcing that the faith is a mystery also mention knowledge of the faith. How do knowledge and mystery fit together when we speak of the faith?

 Stop here and read the following in your own Bible:

- Romans 16:25-26
- Ephesians 1:9-10; 3:1-6, 8-10
- Colossians 1:24-28; 2:1-4; 4:2-4

First, we assert that the mysteries of the faith have been revealed by God in both Scripture and Sacred Tradition. This means that we know many elements of the Christian mysteries — for example, that God is one (Deut 6:4; Mk 12:29) — yet Jesus reveals that the one God is three Persons. At his baptism in the Jordan, the Father speaks, the Son is baptized, and the Holy Spirit hovers over the Son (Mt 3:16-17; Lk 3:21-22). After his resurrection, Jesus teaches the apostles to baptize "in the name of the Father and of the Son and of the Holy Spirit" (Mt 28:19).

The mysterious aspect rests in maintaining these elements of revelation. How is God both one and three Persons at the same time? How is Jesus both God and man? How do humans have free will and yet God's grace saves them?

HERESY

 The word "heresy" comes from a Greek word meaning to take a part out of the whole.

Heretics always take out one component of a mystery, thereby attempting to make it clearer, more understandable, and more logical to the human mind. The mystery of the faith, therefore, is no longer a problem. The Catholic approach is to hold all that God has revealed in the mysteries and profess faith in them.

One image to understand how to maintain orthodox faith in, say, the idea of God being three Persons in one God, is a railroad track: two parallel rails are kept in proper tension by ties so that a train can move forward without mishap. Similarly, the oneness of God and threeness of Persons are kept in tension as parallel lines of thought. The life of faith moves forward along these two lines. If either line is removed, the train of faith is wrecked, and the soul does not reach its destination in the truth of God.

Another important characteristic of the mysteries of the faith is that they come from God and concern God. As such, they are infinite mysteries, as God is infinite. Enough of the mystery is revealed to intrigue the human mind, yet there is always an elusive quality to it. This intrigue will fascinate the human mind, heart, and soul, not only throughout the whole of life on earth but even beyond it into eternity in heaven. For all eternity, these mysteries will remain fascinating, drawing the soul to ever-greater knowledge and wisdom. Never will the soul become sated with God's mysteries. The mysteries of the faith are not like mystery novels that are solved and then put away. Instead, forever will we be drawn into the mysteries of God, and they will give us joy for all eternity.

CONSIDER

The Christian life begins with giving assent to the mysteries of the faith. At Baptism, the priest or deacon poses questions:

> Do you believe in God, the Father almighty, creator of heaven and earth? Do you believe in Jesus Christ, his only Son, our Lord, who was born of the Virgin Mary, was crucified, died,

and was buried, rose from the dead, and is now seated at the right hand of the Father? Do you believe in the Holy Spirit, the holy catholic Church, the communion of saints, the forgiveness of sins, the resurrection of the body, and life everlasting? (see Rite of Baptism for Children, n. 95)

The candidate for Baptism or the sponsor responds "I do" to each query about the faith. Of course, most Catholics are baptized in infancy and the questions were answered for them. The Catholic Church remedies this situation each Easter by including these baptismal promises in the liturgy. Instead of professing the Creed, on Easter the celebrant poses the very questions of the baptismal liturgy to the whole congregation in order to evoke a response of faith from everyone. This means that at each stage of life, in every year we live, we get the opportunity to renew our baptismal promises and once again affirm the fundamental elements of the mysteries of our faith.

Every other Sunday of the year, and on solemnities, the Church asks the Catholic to renew the act of faith in the mysteries of revelation by proclaiming the Nicene Creed. Each one of us states personally, "Credo" (that is, "I believe"), and then pronounces the doctrines about God the Father, the Son, the Holy Spirit, salvation, and the Church. Weekly, we renew the commitment of faith in these doctrines.

INVESTIGATE

THE CREED AND SCRIPTURE

 Look up the following Scripture quotes underlying each statement of the Creed. Pray for God's grace to make ever-deeper commitments to these mysteries and to come to know God more intimately through them:

I believe in one God, (Deut 6:4; Mk 12:29; Eph 4:6; Jas 2:19)

the Father almighty, (Gen 17:1; Eph 4:6)

maker of heaven and earth, (Gen 1:1; Is 40:28)

of all things visible and invisible. (Col 1:16)

I believe in one Lord Jesus Christ, (Eph 4:5; Phil 2:11)

the Only Begotten (Jn 1:14, 18; 3:16; 1 Jn 4:9) **Son of God,**
(2 Cor 1:19)

born of the Father before all ages. (Jn 17:24)

God from God, (Jn 17:3; 1 Jn 5:20) **Light from Light,** (Jn 1:4-9;
1 Jn 1:5,)

true God from true God, (Jn 17:3; 1 Jn 5:20)

begotten, not made, (Heb 1:5) **consubstantial with the Father;**
(Jn 10:30; 14:10-11)

through him all things were made. (Jn 1:1-3; Eph 3:9)

For us men and for our salvation (Jn 12:47; Rom 1:16)

he came down from heaven, (Jn 16:28)

and by the Holy Spirit was incarnate (Lk 1:35) **of the Virgin Mary,**
(Lk 1:30-31)

and became man. (Phil 2:7-8; Heb 2:16)

For our sake he was crucified under Pontius Pilate, (Jn 19:15-16;
Acts 13:28; 1 Tim 6:13)

he suffered death (Jn 19:30; Acts 17:2-3; Heb 2:18; 1 Pet 2:21) **and
was buried,** (Mt 27:59-60; Mk 15:46; Lk 23:53; Jn 19:41-42)

and rose again on the third day

in accordance with the Scriptures. (Ps 16:10; Hos 6:2; Mt 28:6;
Mk 16:6; Lk 24:6-7; 1 Cor 15:3-4)

He ascended into heaven (Acts 1:9)

and is seated at the right hand of the Father. (Lk 22:69; Acts 7:55-
56; Col 3:1; Heb 1:3; 1 Pet 3:22)

He will come again in glory (Mt 24:30; Mk 13:26; Lk 21:27)

to judge the living and the dead (2 Tim 4:1; 1 Pet 4:5; Rev 20:12)

and his kingdom will have no end. (Lk 1:33)

I believe in the Holy Spirit, (Jn 14:26) **the Lord,** (2 Cor 3:17) **the giver of life,** (Jn 3:5)

who proceeds from the Father and the Son, (Jn 14:26; 15:26; 16:14-15)

who with the Father and the Son is adored and glorified, (Mt 28:19; 1 Jn 5:7)

who has spoken through the prophets. (2 Pet 1:21)

I believe in one, (Eph 4:5) **holy,** (Eph 5:27) **catholic** (Col 1:5-6) **and apostolic Church.** (Eph 2:20; Rev 21:14)

I confess one Baptism for the forgiveness of sins (Acts 22:16; Eph 4:5)

and I look forward to the resurrection of the dead (Jn 5:28-29; Acts 24:15)

and the life of the world to come. Amen. (Rev 21:3-5; 22:1-5)

Since profession of the faith is integral to the liturgy throughout the year, we do well to try to understand the faith more and more fully. The more we give ourselves to this understanding, the better we give our whole mind, heart, and soul to the infinite and eternally intriguing God.

DISCUSS

1. Which of the mysteries of the faith is the easiest for you to accept? Which is the most challenging? Why?
2. What connection do you see between faith in the mysteries and your Christian life?
3. What new insight about faith have you received from the Scripture in this chapter?

PRACTICE

This week, do one thing that you find spiritually difficult or challenging, such as forgiving someone who has wronged you, and use it as a way to unite yourself and your struggles with the suffering of Christ for the renewal and redemption of the world.

Session 3

CONVERSION

"The Year of Faith, from this perspective, is a summons to an authentic and renewed conversion to the Lord, the one Savior of the world. In the mystery of his death and Resurrection, God has revealed in its fullness the Love that saves and calls us to conversion of life through the forgiveness of sins (cf. Acts 5:31). For Saint Paul, this Love ushers us into a new life: 'We were buried . . . with him by baptism into death, so that as Christ was raised from the dead by the glory of the Father, we too might walk in newness of life' (Rom 6:4). Through faith, this new life shapes the whole of human existence according to the radical new reality of the Resurrection. To the extent that he freely cooperates, man's thoughts and affections, mentality and conduct are slowly purified and transformed, on a journey that is never completely finished in this life."

— Pope Benedict XVI,
Porta Fidei (n. 6)

The content of faith is very important, whether in the Old Testament, the New Testament, or throughout the history of the Church. The reason is that human beings are created to crave the truth. For someone to commit himself or herself to the faith, he or she must believe that it is true. That belief in and commitment to the faith lies at the heart of Pope Benedict's call to "an authentic and renewed conversion."

However, there is a risk that maintaining true doctrine can become a purely intellectual exercise. One can memorize the dogmas and assent to them, and then hold them in a mental compartment that is not integrated into the rest of life. The Christian act of faith includes intellectual assent to doctrines that are true, but it is much more.

The human person includes the intellect as a component of life that distinguishes humans from the other animals. The mind knows facts and organizes them into meaningful ideas. The better developed the mind is, the more it can recognize the options available to it. However, the will is that distinctive function of the human person that is able to make choices among the various options that the mind sees. The will can choose goals and objectives for the person to achieve, and then it makes choices that the mind can identify best to meet those objectives.

The conscience is a moral voice at the deepest core of the person. The conscience responds to the rudimentary elements of the natural law that God has placed within it — its most basic formulation being, "Do not do to others what you do not want them to do to you." Still, the conscience is capable of much formation and refinement in regard to moral issues. The intellect can form the conscience to know more about basic natural law so that the mind knows how to respond to various moral situations and inform the will to make good moral choices.

CONSIDER

Another key to understanding human beings is the social and interpersonal component of life. Every human is born in a social context — a father and a mother form the bare minimum to make a birth possible, even in those circumstances where either one or the other, or both, abandon a child. The norm is for parents to not only beget and bear a child but also to love, cherish, and raise him or her. We are made to relate to others, involving our emotions, physical life, intellect, conscience, and moral decisions by the will.

The reason to enumerate these various components of the human person — intellect, will, conscience, and relationships — is to highlight that the act of faith includes and affects all of them. The whole person gives himself or herself to God in the act of faith. We commonly describe major acts of faith as conversions, a term referring to the way a person turns around his or her life to believe in God and let that faith change one's whole way of life.

A common image for conversion begins with a person setting out on a path of life. Unfortunately, the path may be a wrong one, so it leads to a variety of mistakes, pain to self and others, disasters, and ultimately death. As the pathway becomes more miserable, the person realizes that it is the wrong way to go. However, the simple realization that the path is wrong is not enough action to constitute a conversion. Assessing that the path is a wrong one does no one any good if the person either continues to walk the same path to destruction or if the individual simply stays put on the destructive path without moving forward or backward.

Two actions are necessary for a conversion to take place. First, the person must believe that a good path to a beneficial and healthy goal exists. Second, he or she must turn around from the bad direction, retrace the steps along the bad path, and then find the good one. In other words, the whole person must undo the wrong decisions and then set out to find the good way. Faith is the act of believing that there is a good path to take through life. Faith in God not only believes that God has created a good path to the ultimate goal of eternal life with him in heaven, but it believes that God will direct us to that right path and strengthen us to walk in it all the way to its completion in eternity.

STUDY

The New Testament offers us a number of examples of people who hear Jesus Christ's call and follow him. Let us examine some of these, and try to see ourselves in one or the other of them.

Simon Peter

Luke 5:1-11 occurs in the context of Jesus' continuing and growing ministry of preaching to the crowds in Galilee. Using his knowledge of nature — namely, the fact that sound travels better over water than land — he asks Simon to put his fishing boat out a little from shore so that the crowds can hear him better.

The end of that sermon begins the call of Simon. First, Jesus tells Simon to "put out into the deep and let down your nets for a catch" (Lk 5:4). This order is contrary to normal fishing practice, which was done at night when fish cannot see the net lowering over them. Though Simon objects, based on his expertise as a fisherman, he acquiesces to accept Jesus' word.

Second, the catch of fish is far beyond natural events — in what was Simon's greatest catch ever, two boats are filled with fish to the point of sinking.

Third, Simon Peter is so frightened by this success that he falls down at Jesus' knees and pleads, "Depart from me, for I am a sinful man, O Lord" (Lk 5:8). Jesus responds to him, "Do not be afraid; henceforth you will be catching men" (Lk 5:10). Then Simon and his partners leave their boats and follow Jesus.

Notice that Simon's recognition of his unworthiness to be in Jesus' presence in the boat leads to repentance. He is not portrayed as a particularly notorious sinner, yet he is aware that even his ordinary sins make him unworthy to be with Jesus.

Simon allowed Jesus' response — "Do not be afraid" — to touch him. This is often said by angels to the people to whom they are sent because the divine both attracts and frightens people. The allaying of Simon's fear opens him to Jesus' invitation to become a fisher of men. Simon chooses to follow Jesus and begins an adventure that not only changes his own life but also the history of the world.

INVESTIGATE

SIMON PETER

No one else is mentioned in the New Testament more than Simon Peter, except for Jesus Christ. It can be instructive to read the four Gospels and the Acts of the Apostles with the view of seeing the various ramifications of Simon's acceptance of Jesus' invitation to follow him that day. Read and make notes on some of the following passages.

PASSAGE	NOTES
Matthew 14:23-33	
Matthew 18:21-35	
Matthew 19:27-30	
Matthew 26:33-41	
Acts 2:14-43	
Acts 4:1-23	
Acts 5:1-16	

STUDY

Matthew

As recorded in Matthew 9:9-13, Jesus saw a tax collector named Matthew. He was sitting at the tax office on the main road passing through Capernaum, the last town in Herod's territory before this major road to Damascus entered the territory of his brother Philip.

Tax collectors were doubly disliked: they collected money for the Roman overlords, causing many people to consider them traitors; and they made their living by keeping any money collected over and above the amount imposed on them by the Roman government, causing some people to consider them thieves. They often became wealthy at the expense of their neighbors, and so they were hated. Pharisees were forbidden to marry into a family that had a tax collector as a member. Nonetheless, Jesus said to Matthew, "Follow me" (Mt 9:9), and Matthew rose and followed him.

Consider the act of faith that Matthew was making by leaving behind the money and career he could see for a journey through life with a poor, itinerant rabbi. He made an amazing act of trust in Jesus that led him to follow Jesus for the next three years and then to go out and preach the Gospel to the world beyond Palestine.

One memorable event in the call of Matthew was its follow-up that evening. Matthew brought Jesus home for a meal. This was extra shocking to the decent people of Capernaum because Matthew also invited the other tax collectors and sinners to the meal. The Pharisees were duly scandalized, but they complained about it to the disciples rather than going to Jesus directly. Jesus himself answered them: "Those who are well have no need of a physician, but those who are sick. Go and learn what this means, 'I desire mercy, and not sacrifice.' For I came not to call the righteous, but sinners" (Mt 9:12-13).

Jesus' response flew in the face of a doctrine of some Pharisees according to which the Messiah would come if every Jew obeyed every commandment of God for a half hour. This meant that each sinner was preventing the arrival of the Messiah. Jesus, on the other hand, taught that it was precisely the sinner who evoked the coming of the Messiah. His presence was not a reward for good behavior but a remedy for it.

This episode shows that the conversion of one sinner can draw one to seek out other sinners to come meet Jesus and discover that faith in him leads to mercy and reconciliation for anyone who trusts in him in faith. Mercy is meant to spread, as sinners invite other sinners to know Jesus Christ.

CONSIDER

Bartimaeus

Another episode of conversion occurs at Jericho when a blind beggar named Bartimaeus heard that Jesus of Nazareth was passing by, as recorded in Mark 10:46-52. The beggar cried out, "Jesus, Son of David, have mercy on me!" (Mk 10:47). Obviously, Bartimaeus had heard about Jesus, and whatever the blind man had heard in the public report about Jesus stirred up faith in him. His faith in Jesus was so confident that when the crowd ordered him to be quiet, he cried out all the louder, "Son of David, have mercy on me!" (Mk 10:48). Note that Bartimaeus addressed Jesus as the Son of David, which means that he understood Jesus to be the fulfillment of the messianic promises of the Old Testament. Still, his faith went beyond that intellectual assent to the truth about Jesus, so he asserted an act of trust in Jesus' mercy for him in his difficult, even impossible, situation of blindness.

Stop here and read the prophecies that the Messiah would come from the descendants of King David in your own Bible. Look up **2 Samuel 7:12-16**; **Psalms 89:29-37**; **Psalms 132:11-12**; **Isaiah 9:6-7**; **11:1-10**. How would you link these prophecies with the genealogy of Jesus in **Matthew 1:1-17**?

Bartimaeus' trust in Jesus was warranted; Jesus halted his journey to Jerusalem and said, "Call him" (Mk 10:49). Note Bartimaeus' eagerness to come to Jesus: he threw off his cloak, sprang up, and went to Jesus (Mk 10:50). When Jesus met him, Jesus asked what he wanted. Bartimaeus replied, "Master, let me receive my sight" (Mk 10:51). The request was bold; granting sight to the blind was not a common occurrence. This bold request indicates Bartimaeus' level of faith in Jesus.

Jesus responded, "Go your way; your faith has made you well" (Mk 10:52). Our Lord's answer indicates how important trustful faith is to him. This bold confidence of trust in Jesus opened Bartimaeus' eyes in two ways. The obvious opening is the physical healing. No longer would Bartimaeus need to beg, but he could take entirely new initiatives in living his life.

The second opening of Bartimaeus' eyes appears in his response. Even though Jesus told him to go his way, Bartimaeus chose to follow Jesus. Though he could not know it at that moment, his following of Jesus would lead to the adventure of a lifetime. Bartimaeus followed Jesus from Jericho to Jerusalem, about twenty miles away. He would be with the crowd for the Palm Sunday entrance into the city and the cleansing of the Temple. He was there for the days of Jesus' teaching and the controversies with the Pharisees and Sadducees. He might well have been there during Jesus' crucifixion and may have remained until the Resurrection.

Bartimaeus is a model for the process of conversion. Conversion requires strong faith such as Bartimaeus had. It becomes a trusting following of Jesus, staying with him to know his teaching and to be formed by it. The convert may have to confront controversies because of Jesus and his teaching, but he or she stays with him, trusting in his wisdom. Most importantly, the convert stays with Jesus at the cross, hearing there the words, "Father, forgive them; for they know not what they do" (Lk 23:34). In this, the individual finds the power to have sins forgiven through all that Christ suffered. Then also, the Resurrection gives the promise of new life, and the convert is nourished and given hope through it.

STUDY

The Samaritan Woman

After some time in the region of Judea, Jesus and the disciples make the return journey to Galilee. Their path goes through the hostile territory of the Samaritans, where Jesus and the disciples decide to rest. While the disciples go to procure food, a Samaritan woman comes to draw water at noon — an odd time of day since most women came for water early in the morning and again in the evening. Jesus says to her, "Give me a drink" (Jn 4:7).

 In *Porta Fidei* (n. 3), Pope Benedict mentions the conversion of the Samaritan woman in **John 4:1-42**. Stop here and read this passage in your own Bible.

Her response addresses the issue of Jewish and Samaritan hostility: "How is it that you, a Jew, ask a drink of me, a woman of Samaria?" (Jn 4:9). As if he cares nothing about that ethnic and religious dispute, Jesus answers her: "If you knew the gift of God, and who it is that is saying to you, 'Give me a drink,' you would have asked him and he would have given you living water" (Jn 4:10). His answer is meant not so much as a response to the information she has requested as it is a vehicle of drawing her into a topic that is more profound and important than mere water, while still using the terms about water.

The woman has no way of knowing that Jesus is speaking about deeper spiritual issues, so she answers on the natural level: "Sir, you have nothing to draw with, and the well is deep; where do you get that living water? Are you greater than our father Jacob, who gave us the well, and drank from it himself, and his sons, and his cattle?" (Jn 4:11-12).

Jesus answers neither of these questions directly but responds with a call to still deeper meaning: "Everyone who drinks of this water will thirst again, but whoever drinks of the water that I shall give him will never thirst; the water that I shall give him will become in him a spring of water welling up to eternal life" (Jn 4:13-14).

Jesus' concern is not limited to the physical need to quench the body's thirst but moves to the deepest concerns of human existence. Humans have a thirst for the ultimate meaning and purpose of life, and he wants to satisfy that longing. St. Augustine's famous line from the *Confessions*, "Our hearts are restless until they rest in Thee," poetically expresses that longing. Furthermore, as is the case throughout the Gospel, Jesus offers faith in eternal life as the response to the fear of death that is part of human life. Nearly everyone confronts the fact that life is short compared to the eternity that continues after a person is dead.

The woman answers Jesus' offer with eagerness, though one cannot help but think that she is still seeking physical, perhaps magical, water to satisfy her bodily needs for fluids: "Sir, give me this water, that I may not thirst, nor come here to draw" (Jn 4:15).

Jesus takes the conversation to a new, more personal level by telling her, "Go, call your husband, and come here" (Jn 4:16). When she responds, "I have no husband," Jesus agrees. "You are right in saying, 'I have no husband'; for you have had five husbands, and he whom you now have is not your husband; this you said truly" (4:17-18). He could have called her a liar and an immoral woman who cannot admit to her sins when she is caught, but he does not. Rather, he agrees with the literal statement she has made and then expands on it with the rest of the truth about her life. This is an important aspect of coming to God in conversion; he knows us better than we know ourselves, and more thoroughly than we are willing to admit to ourselves. For this reason, the process of conversion entails a thorough examination of conscience. The saints point out that the more a person comes to know Christ, the deeper the repentance becomes because humans come to see themselves more clearly in the light of Christ.

The woman's response to Jesus' revelation about her life is twofold. On the one hand, she subtly admits that he is right when she says, "Sir, I perceive that you are a prophet" (Jn 4:19). She does not yet know how to integrate this knowledge, so she changes the subject to a more theoretical, theological issue: "Our fathers worshiped on this mountain; and you say that in Jerusalem is the place where men ought to worship" (Jn 4:20). While concern for the truth of a situation is important, people need to be alert that theological disputes can be used as dodges to the personal issues of conversion. How does Jesus handle this?

Here he responds with a direct answer to her question. First, he gives a promise that worship will be neither along Samaritan nor traditional Jewish patterns: "Woman, believe me, the hour is coming when neither on this mountain nor in Jerusalem will you worship the Father" (Jn 4:21). The idea of worshiping God as Father will be new and unexpected to her. Addressing God as Father is not part of Samaritan theology.

THE SAMARITANS

The Samaritans lived in the central highlands of Israel near Shechem, which is found near the present-day West Bank City of Nablus. The Samaritans considered themselves the descendants of the tribes of Manasseh and Ephraim; Jews considered them descendants of Israelites who survived the Assyrian conquest of 721 B.C., with a mixture of Gentiles who were brought in by the Assyrians as settlers. When the Jews returned from Babylon and finished their new temple in 515 B.C., the Samaritans felt unwelcome and built their own temple in the early fifth century B.C. Tension existed for centuries, with a number of violent outbreaks between them in the first centuries B.C. and A.D.

Second, Jesus states a truth about the history of salvation, since the woman has recognized him as a prophet who speaks God's truth: "You worship what you do not know; we worship what we know, for salvation is from the Jews" (Jn 4:22). Since salvation history is from the Jews, then Jesus, a Jew, can be the vehicle to bring that salvation to the world.

Third, Jesus returns to his point about the new dispensation he is inaugurating in regard to authentic worship: "But the hour is coming, and now is, when the true worshipers will worship the Father in spirit and truth, for such the Father seeks to worship him. God is spirit, and those who worship him must worship in spirit and truth" (Jn 4:23-24). Because God is spirit, he will not be limited to the Samaritan temple on Mount Gerizim (where it still exists) nor to the Jewish Temple in Jerusalem. God will be worshiped in spirit and truth wherever people know the truth.

The woman redirects the conversation once more: "I know that Messiah is coming (he who is called Christ); when he comes, he will show us all things" (Jn 4:25). She obviously already has faith in the all-knowing Messiah of the future. This is her response to Jesus' strong assertion about authentic worship in the future. Then, for the first time in the Gospel of John, Jesus clearly states: "I who speak to you am he" (Jn 4:26). He professes to be not merely a prophet but the Messiah who knows all things, whether they concern her personal life or her theological questions.

At this juncture in the conversation, two things happen. The disciples return to the well, marveling that Jesus was speaking with a woman (Jn 4:27). Then the woman runs back to the city and tells her fellow citizens about Jesus: "Come, see a man who told me all that I ever did. Can this be the Christ?" (Jn 4:29). Her profession of faith is a question she poses to them, but it is based on her experience of being told about her own sins. As her attitude to her past has become one of integrating the sinful facts that everyone in town already knows, they come out to see Jesus (Jn 4:30).

The situation also becomes an occasion for conversion for the disciples. While they want him to eat food, he says, "I have food to eat of which you do not know. . . . My food is to do the will of him who sent me, and to accomplish his work" (Jn 4:32, 34). If Jesus is nourished by doing the Father's will, then they must learn to seek the same food. That means that they will be sent by Jesus to win many souls for the kingdom of heaven (Jn 4:35-38).

Meanwhile, the Samaritans come to believe in Jesus "because of the woman's testimony, 'He told me all that I ever did' " (Jn 4:39). Then, the longer Jesus stays with them, the more they come to believe in him "because of his word" (Jn 4:41). They tell the woman, "It is no longer because of your words that we believe, for we have heard for ourselves, and we know that this is indeed the Savior of the world" (Jn 4:42). The fruit of this visit can be seen later, in Acts 8:1-25, when the deacon Philip and then the apostles Peter and John evangelize in Samaria.

INVESTIGATE

CONVERSION STORIES

 There are many conversion stories to look at in the New Testament. Consider how faith in Jesus changed the lives of the following people:

- Luke 19:1-10 — Zacchaeus
- John 9:1-41 — a man born blind (especially verses 35-38)
- Acts 8:26-40 — the Ethiopian eunuch
- Acts 9:1-22 — Saul
- Acts 10:1-48 — Cornelius
- Acts 16:11-15 — Lydia
- Acts 16:25-34 — the jailer in Philippi

Christian faith believes that Jesus Christ personifies the way we must take ("I am the way" [Jn 14:6]). Christians commit themselves to Jesus Christ and follow him in a close personal union by the power of his grace. However, this is a process that requires daily commitment and conversion. As St. Richard of Wyche prayed in the thirteenth century: "O most merciful redeemer, friend, and brother, may I know thee more clearly, love thee more dearly, and follow thee more nearly, day by day."

DISCUSS

1. Blindness isn't always physical. How might you be blind to your own faults or sins?
2. What do you think are the key elements in the process of conversion? What role does faith play?
3. What new insight about faith have I received from the Scriptures in this chapter?

PRACTICE

This week, ask Jesus to help you see what needs to be changed in your life in order for a true conversion to take place, and then ask him for the courage to act upon your insights.

Session 4

THE WITNESS OF CHARITY

Jesus had a most intriguing encounter with a woman while dining at the home of Simon the Pharisee (Lk 7:36-50). The woman brought an expensive alabaster jar of ointment, washed Jesus' feet with her tears, wiped them with her hair, kissed them, and anointed them with her precious ointment (Lk 7:37-38).

Stop here and read **Luke 7:36-50** in your own Bible.

The Pharisees at table used the situation to doubt Jesus' prophetic powers, since he showed no recognition that the woman was a publicly known sinner (Lk 7:39). Jesus, at first, responded to the unspoken criticism by asking Simon, his host, to explain a parable about two debtors — one owing five hundred denarii and the other owing fifty — whose debts were forgiven. Simon correctly answered that the one whose larger debt was forgiven would love the creditor more than the other debtor (Lk 7:40-43). Jesus then applied the parable to the repentant woman. First, he contrasted her acts of kindness with the lack of these signs of hospitality from his more respectable Pharisee host (Lk 7:44-47). Second, Jesus explained, "Therefore I tell you, her sins, which are many, are forgiven, for she loved much; but he who is forgiven little, loves little" (Luke 7:47). Third, Jesus turned to the woman and shocked the other guests by taking explicitly divine authority to reconcile sinners, saying, "Your sins are forgiven" (Lk 7:48). Fourth, Jesus ignored the outrage over his forgiving her sins and told the woman, "Your faith has saved you; go in peace" (Lk 7:50).

It is significant to see that Jesus stated that the many sins of the woman were forgiven because she loved much (Lk 7:47) and then told her that her faith saved her (Lk 7:50). In this passage, Jesus linked faith and love in a particular way.

CONSIDER

St. Paul, who was converted from arresting Christians so as to execute them, came to believe profoundly in the power of Christ's death to reconcile sinners:

God shows his love for us in that while we were yet sinners Christ died for us. Since, therefore, we are now justified by his blood, much more shall we be saved by him from the wrath of God. For if while we were enemies we were reconciled to God by the death of his Son, much more, now that we are reconciled, shall we be saved by his life. (Rom 5:8-10)

 Stop here and read in your own Bible the following passages that show St. Paul's drive to demonstrate his love of Christ as the central force of his life:

- **Romans 8:31-39**
- **2 Corinthians 4:7-18; 11:16-33**
- **Ephesians 3:1-13**
- **Philippians 2:14-18; 3:1-16**
- **Colossians 1:24-25**
- **2 Timothy 1:1-18**

He came to know the depth of forgiveness in Christ, and he spent the rest of his life preaching about Jesus and winning people to him. Nothing else was important to St. Paul. He believed in Jesus and loved Jesus, and consequently he loved humanity.

CONSIDER

Faith in God is about the many things the Lord has done for humanity. Faith believes God has acted in the history of Israel to form a people and prepare them with saving deeds and prophecies to bring the Savior to the whole world. Faith believes the many truths about Jesus in the Gospel. However, when we gain perspective on these truths of faith, we see that God has done all this because he loves us. He offers us unconditional love, and it is up to us to respond.

The proper response is to obey the two great commandments: first, that we love God with our whole heart, mind, and soul (Deut 6:5; Mt 22:37; Mk 12:30; Lk 10:27-28); then Jesus adds the second commandment, which is to love our neighbor as ourself (Lev 19:18; Mt 22:39; Mk 12:31; Lk 10:27-28).

STUDY

In Galatians, St. Paul emphasizes that faith in Jesus Christ and his saving death, not obedience to the precepts of the Mosaic Law, will give us eternal life. Though he rejects works of the Law as the way to justification, he writes, "For in Christ Jesus neither circumcision nor uncircumcision is of any avail, but faith working through love" (Gal 5:6). Clearly, Paul does not isolate faith from love but sees that faith is directed to love.

Romans is another epistle that makes faith a central theme.

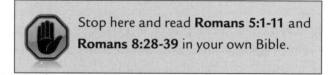

Stop here and read **Romans 5:1-11** and **Romans 8:28-39** in your own Bible.

First, St. Paul summarizes the discussion of faith in Romans (chapters 2 through 4) in Romans 5:1-5. The culmination of this paragraph is that "God's love has been poured into our hearts through the Holy Spirit who has been given to us" (Rom 5:5). Read this line in the context of St. Paul describing the grace of faith that leads to hope. Throughout his epistles, St. Paul mentions these three theological virtues (faith, hope, and love) together.

Next, pay close attention to St. Paul's assertion that God's love is poured into us through the Holy Spirit. He does not link love with a feeling or an emotion, but with the active presence of the third Person of the Blessed Trinity — the Holy Spirit. This means that the love within us is a gift of God's own love.

The next paragraph (Rom 5:6-11) responds to the fact of human helplessness to be reconciled to God by making an assertion of faith: "But God shows his love for us in that while we were yet sinners Christ died for us" (Rom 5:8). God's love does not wait for people to become perfect, but instead he loves them while they are still in the midst of their sins.

God's love is not some emotion on his part but the gift of his own Son. The nature of Christian love is to be a gift of oneself and the willingness to accept the one who is loved. God's love accepts sinners in their sinful state but then takes them beyond their limits to become lovers of God and of fellow sinners.

In Romans 8:28-39, St. Paul continues his profound reflection on God's love. First, he asserts, as an act of deep trust in God, that "we know that in everything God works for good with those who love him, who are called according to his purpose" (Rom 8:28). This brings out the need for the believer to respond to God in love. Then he explains that the goal of this love is "to be conformed to the image of his Son, in order that he might be the firstborn among many brethren" (Rom 8:29).

Recall Genesis 1:26, where God created man in his image and likeness. Through the fall into original sin, "all have sinned and fall short of the glory of God" (Rom 3:23). God sent his Son to become flesh in order to restore that image and likeness in one man, Christ the new Adam (see 1 Cor 15:45), and through him to restore all who live the life of faith in him to that image and likeness of God.

In Romans 8:31-34, St. Paul asks a number of rhetorical questions meant to evoke a variety of assertions. God is for us, so no one can really be against us (Rom 8:31). Since God gave up his Son, then he will give us all things (Rom 8:32). No one can bring charges against God's elect (Rom 8:33). Christ Jesus, who died, was raised from the dead, who is at God's right hand, and who intercedes for us, will not condemn us (Rom 8:34). These questions evoke acts of faith and trust.

Then Paul comes back to the love of God and asks about a variety of negative forces in life (Rom 8:35-36) but concludes that none of them can separate us from Christ's love because "we are more than conquerors through him who loved us" (Rom 8:37). Next he asserts that nothing in creation, not even death or angels (Rom 8:38-39), "will be able to separate us from the love of God in Christ Jesus our Lord" (Rom 8:39).

Note how strongly Paul's various acts of faith are firm statements of trust in God no matter how difficult life becomes. His central conclusion is that God's love for us is absolute, so we need fear nothing.

Having established these links between faith and the love of God, St. Paul then includes important exhortations to love our neighbor as well in Romans 12-13.

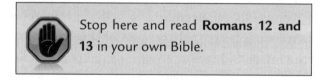

Stop here and read **Romans 12 and 13** in your own Bible.

In these chapters, St. Paul invites Christians to act in love. One aspect of this love is humility — one should not "think of himself more highly than he ought to think, but to think with sober judgment, each according to the measure of faith which God has assigned him" (Rom 12:3).

Second, Paul teaches that the Church is one body with many members, each with his or her own role in the community. Therefore, we are to use the gifts for the sake of the other members of the Church (Rom 12:4-8).

Third, Paul explicitly summons the community to love (Rom 12:9). This love takes a number of concrete forms: "contribute to the needs of the saints, practice hospitality" (Rom 12:13); "bless those who persecute you" (Rom 12:14).

Fourth, in Romans 13:8-10, Paul links love to the commandments. He begins with the principle, "Owe no one anything, except to love one another" (Rom 13:8a). The reason underlying this principle is that "he who loves his neighbor has fulfilled the law" (Rom 13:8b). Then, having cited four of the Ten Commandments, he asserts that all of the commandments "are summed up in this sentence, 'You shall love your neighbor as yourself' " (Rom 13:9). This quote from Leviticus 19:18 is, of course, the same commandment cited by Jesus Christ in Matthew 19:19 and elsewhere. St. Paul explains that "love does no wrong to a neighbor; therefore love is the fulfilling of the law" (Rom 13:10).

INVESTIGATE

FAITH AND WORKS

 In James 2:10-13, St. James teaches Christians to keep the whole Law, and then he mentions some commandments. Compare his list with St. Paul's in Romans 13:8-10 and Jesus' list in Mark 10:18-19, and with the Old Testament list in Exodus 20:1-17 and Deuteronomy 5:6-21. Consider the different audiences in each context, and think about why some commandments are highlighted more than others.

> Stop here and read **James 2:14-26** in your own Bible.

In this famous passage, St. James disputes the question of the relationship between faith and works (Jas 2:14-26). Note that he never rejects faith. Rather, he insists on exhorting Christians to have their faith come alive through good works of charity and love. "So faith by itself, if it has no works, is dead" (Jas 2:17), and "faith apart from works is barren" (Jas 2:20). In a more positive formulation, St. James teaches that "faith was completed by works" (Jas 2:22). "You see that a man is justified by works and not by faith alone" (Jas 2:24).

PELAGIANISM

One error that appeared in the early Church with regard to doing good works is Pelagianism. Pelagius taught that humans can save themselves by their own efforts unaided by grace. St. Augustine championed the orthodox faith by keeping the balance between the necessity of good works and the necessity of God's grace to aid the human will to perform works of love. Love, like faith, is a theological virtue. This means that God's grace is necessary to love; the unaided human will cannot.

CONSIDER

Let us conclude this chapter with yet another New Testament insight about the relation between faith and love — namely, that love increases faith.

Ephesians 3:17-19 is part of St. Paul's prayer for the Ephesian community:

> . . . and that Christ may dwell in your hearts through faith; that you, being rooted and grounded in love, may have power to comprehend with all the saints what is the breadth and length and height and depth, and to know the love of Christ which surpasses knowledge, that you may be filled with all the fulness of God.

The love in verse 17 is twofold: first, it is the dwelling of Christ within us and, second, a rootedness and grounding of the whole of life in love. This double love gives the "power to comprehend with all the saints what is the breadth and length and height and depth" (Eph 3:18) — that is, all the dimensions of the mystery of Christ (see Eph 3:3-6). This love makes it possible to know the love of Christ — again, the grace of love makes love possible. That love of Christ surpasses knowledge and makes it possible for the Christian to "be filled with all the fulness of God" (Eph 3:19).

INVESTIGATE

CHARISMATIC GIFTS

 A favorite chapter on love is 1 Corinthians 13:1-13, which is in the middle of St. Paul's most detailed teaching on the charismatic gifts in the Church, the Body of Christ (1 Cor 12 and 14).

 Stop here and read **1 Corinthians 13:1-13** in your own Bible.

How does St. Paul compare love to the charismatic gifts? How does love compare to faith? knowledge? generosity? prophecies?

_____

_____

_____

Because we believe what Jesus has taught and done, we take the two great commands to love God and neighbor as determinants of the meaning of life. In fact, we come to believe that not only our authentic faith but also our sincere love will be key factors in the way God judges whether we go to heaven or not.

_____

DISCUSS

1. In what ways can you further examine your life to know what is true and false about the ways you love?
2. How can you cooperate with God's gift of love so that you might become a more loving person of faith?
3. What new insight about love have you received from the Scriptures in this chapter?

PRACTICE

Use 1 Corinthians 13:4-7 as a starting point to make an examination of conscience. To make the passage more personal, substitute the words "love is . . ." with the words "I am . . ." (or similar wording). Afterward, make an Act of Contrition and go to confession soon.

Session 5

CELEBRATING FAITH

"We want this Year to arouse in every believer the aspiration to profess the faith in fullness and with renewed conviction, with confidence and hope. It will also be a good opportunity to intensify the celebration of the faith in the liturgy, especially in the Eucharist, which is 'the summit towards which the activity of the Church is directed; . . . and also the source from which all its power flows.' At the same time, we make it our prayer that believers' witness of life may grow in credibility. To rediscover the content of the faith that is professed, celebrated, lived and prayed, and to reflect on the act of faith, is a task that every believer must make his own, especially in the course of this Year."

— Pope Benedict XVI,
Porta Fidei (n. 9)

Faith that is not expressed and celebrated cannot grow. That is why, in *Porta Fidei*, Pope Benedict calls on each of us to use the liturgy, especially the Eucharist, as a way both to profess our faith and to increase it on a regular basis. In this Year of Faith, we are asked, not just to renew our own personal commitment to Jesus, but to join together as the Body of Christ in worshiping the living God, for faith and worship have never been and can never be purely personal matters.

CONSIDER

Throughout the entire story of salvation, as passed down in the Scriptures, worship and faith have been intrinsically linked. Faith typically leads to an expression of worship in which people not only profess their belief, but offer a sacrifice of what is their very best, a symbol of part of their own lives. The narratives come in the context of new experiences of faith in the one God. Abram first heard God speak, and then he offered sacrifice; Jacob heard the renewal of the promise of land and descendants and set up the stone at Bethel with an anointing. Later, Moses met God, learned his name and purpose for Israel, which would be worship at Mount Sinai. Then the worship took place, with sacrifices, after the people professed faith in the words of the Lord.

THE PARTS OF THE MASS

 As Catholics, our worship centers on the Mass. The Mass has a number of parts, each of which is a call to deepen our faith:

Introductory Rites

The Sign of the Cross is both a blessing and a commitment to participate in the whole Eucharist, "In the name of the Father, and of the Son, and of the Holy Spirit." The priest's greeting blesses the congregation to receive the grace of God in order to celebrate the Mass. The congregation can wish this grace back to the priest by saying, "And with your spirit."

Penitential Act

This part of the Mass acknowledges that we have sinned and at the same time expresses faith that the Lord forgives us.

continued on next page…

Doxology (Gloria)

The song of the angels at Bethlehem is expanded into praises of the Blessed Trinity. The words are acts of faith in each Person of the Trinity, with praise and petition interspersed. The act of faith is twofold: doctrine feeds the intellect; petition and trust move the will.

Collect

This is a petition prayer asking God's help to celebrate this particular Mass, focusing on the themes of that liturgy.

Readings

We believe that the readings are the word of God. At the end of each reading, we make a response of faith:

V. The word of the Lord.

R. Thanks be to God.

V. The Gospel of the Lord.

R. Praise to you, Lord Jesus Christ.

The homily continues the readings with a reflection on their meaning for faith. It is less a lecture than an exhortation to believe and apply the faith to life.

Creed

This is a statement of key dogmas of the faith. By reciting it, we are making a personal profession of faith in public.

Offertory

The priest's prayers emphasize that the bread and wine are gifts from God and his providence. The people's response, "Blessed be God for ever," is an act of faithful thanksgiving that we have the gifts

continued on next page…

to offer. The priest asks the congregation to pray that the sacrifice be acceptable, which they do. They express their faith in the power of the priest to offer their sacrifice.

Dialogue and Preface

This prayer to the Father is always a preparation for the canon, petitioning him and asking the help of the angels and saints in our worship.

Sanctus (Holy, Holy, Holy)

This hymn of the seraphim is both promise of God's presence and an act of faith in the coming of the Lord, who will be present in just a few moments.

Canon (Eucharistic Prayer)

This prayer is addressed to the Father, trusting in his goodness. The Holy Spirit is invoked to come upon the gifts and transform them into the Body and Blood of Christ (*epiclesis*). The words of Jesus from the Last Supper are spoken by the priest to effect this transformation from the side of human cooperation. The rest of the prayer consists of petitions for the Church, her leaders, and the living and the dead. The conclusion is the Great Amen, an act of faith by the whole congregation to set its acceptance of all that has gone before.

Our Father

The congregation prays with Jesus, now present on the altar, the prayer he taught us. This is faith in the intimate relationship we have with God as Father, who answers our lofty concern for the coming of the kingdom and his will, the lowly needs for daily bread, and the humble need for forgiveness.

Sign of Peace

This is more than a friendly greeting; it is a prayer for Christ's peace for the congregation.

continued on next page…

Lamb of God

This verse from John the Baptist (Jn 1:29, 36) is an act of faith in Jesus, who is about to enter our hearts as the Lamb of God who takes away sin and brings peace.

Communion

As the priest professes an act of faith to each communicant, "The Body of Christ"/"The Blood of Christ," each one responds back in faith, "Amen."

Post-Communion Prayer

This prayer sums up the faith we have experienced at Mass, especially in receiving the Eucharist.

Blessing and Dismissal

The priest blesses everyone in the name of the Trinity so that all may receive grace before the dismissal to go out into the world and continue living the grace of the Mass.

STUDY

The tragic story of Cain and Abel hinges on their experience of worship — offering sacrifices to God from their crops and flocks. One sacrifice pleases the Lord, but the other does not, driving Cain to become so jealous that he murders his brother Abel (Gen 4:1-16). The next act of worship seen in the Bible occurs when Noah and his family leave the ark. Noah offers a sweet-smelling sacrifice to the Lord that pleases him, and the Lord responds by making a covenant never to flood the entire earth again (Gen 8:20-22; 9:1-17).

The offering of sacrifice becomes more frequent after the Lord calls Abram away from Ur and Haran, where he worshiped pagan deities, to Canaan, where he is converted to have faith in the one

God who created the universe. That summons was both a call and a promise from God: "I will make of you a great nation, and I will bless you, and make your name great, so that you will be a blessing. I will bless those who bless you, and him who curses you I will curse; and by you all the families of the earth shall bless themselves" (Gen 12:2-3).

The promise to make Abram a great nation with a great name is not just for the sake of Abram and his posterity but is a promise for all of the families of the earth. The Lord's blessing on Abram is meant to extend to every other human, and they will bless themselves by Abram, a promise that intimates that the worship of the whole world will be affected by their attitude to Abram.

As soon as Abram arrives in Canaan, he goes to Shechem and builds an altar for worship (Gen 12:5-7). Then he travels near to Bethel and builds another altar (Gen 12:8). Next he moves to the oaks of Mamre, near Hebron, and builds yet another altar (Gen 13:18). After he defeats four kings and saves his nephew Lot, Abram goes to Melchizedek, king of Salem and priest of God Most High, who offers bread and wine for Abram (Gen 14:17-20). When the Lord promises to reward Abram, Abram wants to know how the Lord will fulfill the promise of posterity to such an old man, already around eighty years old. The Lord renews the promise of descendants: "And he believed the Lord; and he reckoned it to him as righteousness" (Gen 15:6). This act of faith is followed by the building of an altar and the offering of sacrifice (Gen 15:7-21).

After the birth of Isaac, the son promised to Abraham (God changed Abram's name when he commanded Abram to be circumcised, as a sign of the covenant as told in Gen 17:1-27) and Sarah, God tests Abraham by asking him to sacrifice Isaac. Abraham obeys, leads Isaac, who is carrying the wood for the sacrifice, to Mount Moriah, ties him up, and lifts the knife to sacrifice the boy. An angel of the Lord stops him. Abraham then sees a ram tangled in a bush and sacrifices the ram instead of Isaac (Gen 22:1-18).

CONSIDER

In Genesis, Jacob has tricked his father Isaac into giving him the family blessing instead of giving it to Esau (Gen 27:1-40). Because Esau wants revenge, Jacob flees to his mother's brother, Laban, in Paddan-aram (Gen 27:41-28:5). On the way, Jacob stops at Bethel, where he dreams of a ladder to heaven, with angels going up and down, bringing petitions up to God and answers back down. When he awakes, he anoints a stone with oil as a sacred pillar and makes a vow: "If God will be with me, and will keep me in this way that I go, and will give me bread to eat and clothing to wear, so that I come again to my father's house in peace, then the Lord shall be my God, and this stone, which I have set up for a pillar, shall be God's house; and of all that you give me I will give the tenth to you" (Gen 28:20-22). This vow is improper because Jacob has established the conditions by which he promises to offer God a sacrifice of a tithe — if God takes care of him, he will worship. God does take care of Jacob while he lives with his uncle: he marries Laban's two daughters and their two slaves; he has thirteen children with them; and he becomes a wealthy owner of flocks.

However, just before Jacob returns to Canaan with his family and wealth, he wrestles with God's angel, who injures his hip. This occurs to let Jacob know that while God may have answered Jacob's requests in the vow at Bethel, God is still in charge of the relationship, not Jacob (Gen 32:22-32).

STUDY

In Exodus 3, the Lord again takes the initiative to call a man, this time Moses. A burning bush attracts Moses, but as he approaches it, the voice of God requires him to remove his shoes because the ground is holy due to God's presence (Ex 3:3-5). Then the voice identifies himself: "I am the God of your father, the God of Abraham, the God of Isaac, and the God of Jacob" (Ex 3:6). God's purpose in appearing to Moses is to instruct him to deliver Israel from Egypt and to bring them to Canaan, the land promised to the ancestors (Ex 3:7-10). Moses objects to this assignment by saying, "Who am I?" (Ex 3:11). Then God responds, "But I will be with you; and this shall be the sign for you, that I have sent you: when you have brought forth the people out of Egypt, you shall serve God upon this mountain" (Ex 3:12). This is a double promise: to be with Moses and to bring Israel out of Egypt to worship on Mount Sinai. Moses is to have faith in God's presence and then lead the people in a worshipful response. This means that worship is a purpose not only for the Exodus but also for life in the Promised Land.

After all the crises of the Exodus, the Israelites arrive at Mount Sinai, where they worship just as God said they would. At this point, six things happen. First, Moses presents God's offer of a covenant to the people, and they accept the offer (Ex 19:3-9, with the liturgical response in 19:8, "All that the Lord has spoken we will do"). Second, the Lord asks Moses to consecrate the people by cleaning their garments (not so easy in the desert), refraining from sexual union, and respecting the sacredness of Mount Sinai (Ex 19:10-15). Third, the Lord comes down to the mountain, bringing fear on the people and summoning Moses to meet him (Ex 19:16-17). Fourth, God gives Moses the Ten Commandments and other laws (Ex 20-23), determining the moral quality of life the Israelites must have in order to be his people. Fifth, Moses returns to the people with the Law and lets them hear it and give a communal acceptance of it (Ex 24:1-4a, especially 24:3, which they do by saying, "All the words which the Lord has spoken we will do"). Sixth, Moses builds an altar, sacrifices twelve bulls, one from each tribe, pours out the blood on the altar and the people (Ex 24:4b-8), followed by a sacrificial meal on the mountain (Ex 24:9-11).

INVESTIGATE

THE PROMISED LAND'S FIRST SHRINE

 The Book of Joshua contains a number of liturgical events. Joshua 4:19-24 describes the first shrine in the Promised Land at Gilgal, where the people set up twelve stones from the Jordan River, then circumcised the men (Josh 5:1-9), and offered the Passover (Josh 5:10-12). Then Joshua 24 relates a covenant renewal to commit Israel to the Lord.

CONSIDER

The Gospels begin by assuming the liturgical life of Israel. Jesus is circumcised (Lk 2:21) and presented in the Temple with a sacrifice (Lk 2:22-38); the Holy Family goes to Jerusalem yearly for Passover (Lk 2:41); and Jesus continues this during his public ministry (Mt 26:1-5; Mk 14:1-2; Lk 22:1-2; Jn 2:13; 11:55-56; 13:1), as well as for the feast of Tabernacles (Jn 7:2, 10-14). This shows that Jesus lived in continuity with the Old Testament liturgical worship.

A major development in New Testament liturgy occurs at the last Passover mentioned in the Gospel, when Jesus adds a whole new component to the Jewish ritual. He takes the unleavened matzah, gives thanks, blesses it, breaks it, and gives it to his apostles at table, saying, "This is my body which is given for you" (Lk 22:19). Then he takes the cup and says, "This chalice which is poured out for you is the new covenant in my blood" (Lk 22:20).

By this action, Jesus has redefined the Passover, from the celebration of Israel's deliverance from Egypt into the world's deliverance from sin. The Eucharist is linked to Christ offering his body and blood on the cross: "For as often as you eat this bread and drink the chalice, you proclaim the Lord's death until he comes" (1 Cor 11:26). Those who have faith in him accept this new sense and understand it as a new covenant, as we see in Matthew 26:27-28: "Drink of it, all of you; for this is my blood of the covenant, which is poured out for many for the forgiveness of sins." This new liturgical action by Jesus is so important that he tells the disciples, "Do this in remembrance of me" (Lk 22:19), a command by which he ordains the priests of this new covenant so that the new sign of God's love can be repeated throughout the life of the Church.

STUDY

A key to understanding Jesus' new liturgy is the discourse in John 6:22-71. It begins with Jesus rebuking the crowd that wanted mere food that perishes instead of food for eternal life (Jn 6:26-27). Then he explains, "This is the work of God, that you believe in him whom he has sent" (Jn 6:29). Jesus treats faith as essential for understanding his teaching.

Stop here and read **John 6:22-71** in your own Bible.

Next, Jesus introduces the topic that "I am the bread of life; he who comes to me shall not hunger, and he who believes in me shall never thirst. . . . For this is the will of my Father, that every one who sees the Son and believes in him should have eternal life; and I will raise him up at the last day" (Jn 6:35, 40). Jesus claims to personify the bread of life and demands faith in himself in order to give life.

He further explains, "I am the living bread which came down from heaven; if any one eats of this bread, he will live for ever; and the bread which I shall give for the life of the world is my flesh" (Jn 6:51). His claim does not evoke faith among the listeners but shock. Jesus' response to their shock is "unless you eat the flesh of the Son of man and drink his blood, you have no life in you; he who eats my flesh and drinks my blood has eternal life, and I will raise him up at the last day" (Jn 6:53-54). This statement then elicits dissent among Jesus' own disciples, so he responds that his words are "Spirit and life. But there are some of you that do not believe" (Jn 6:63-64). Jesus even asks the Twelve if they want to leave, but Peter expresses faith: "Lord, to whom shall we go? You have the words of eternal life; and we have believed, and have come to know, that you are the Holy One of God" (Jn 6:68-69). From beginning to end, faith is essential in this whole discourse.

This passage explains the meaning of Jesus' new liturgy at the Last Supper, when he takes bread and declares it to be his body and takes wine and declares it to be his blood. Jesus gives them to the apostles so that they can have eternal life. He commands them to "do this" so that they can bring eternal life to the rest of the world. Jesus simply requires people to believe in him and his words, and in particular to believe that he truly gives his flesh and blood so that they might have eternal life.

The Acts of the Apostles shows that the early Christians continued worshiping in the Temple, much as Jesus had done. Yet Jesus' new ritual was also practiced by these Christians from the beginning of the Church: "All who believed were together . . . attending the temple together and breaking bread in their homes, they partook of food with glad and generous hearts, praising God and having favor with all the people" (Acts 2:44, 46-47).

CONSIDER

The "breaking of the bread" was St. Luke's term for the Eucharist. Of course, this was practiced not only by the Jerusalem Christians but also throughout all of the communities (see Acts 20:7 and 1 Cor 11:23-26). The early Fathers of the Church also attest to the Eucharistic celebrations as well. The structure of the Eucharist was influenced by Jewish ceremonies, especially from the synagogue and Temple. Readings from Scripture preceded the celebration of the "breaking of the bread." Other Mass prayers come from the synagogue service — for example, the dialogue:

V. The Lord be with you.

R. **And with your spirit.**

V. Lift up your hearts.

R. **We lift them up to the Lord.**

V. Let us give thanks to the Lord our God.

R. **It is right and just.**

In the synagogue, this dialogue is followed by the "Holy, Holy, Holy Lord God of hosts" — a quote from Isaiah 6:3, where the seraphim sing this hymn (see also Rev 4:8).

Later Christians continued to develop the prayers of the liturgy in different parts of the world and in different languages. The amazing aspect of this is not the diversity in the liturgies but the similarity of structure throughout the various rites. Eventually, these prayers became set and normative within each rite of the Church, bestowing structure to the liturgy.

A couple of advantages adhere to this process of structuring the liturgy. First, and perhaps more obvious, the set structure allows the whole community to know what to expect in the liturgy and how to participate in it. Prayers and their expected responses can be memorized so that the whole community joins in communal participation at the appropriate moments.

A second reason for the set structure in the liturgy is that it refines the various expressions of faith in each prayer. The words of the celebrant and congregation can put the faith into prayer forms. These words keep a balance among the various truths of the faith, and they exclude formulas that contradict the faith. These prayers can serve to teach doctrine while the community is worshiping. They remind everyone of the various teachings of the faith, particularly in the Creed.

THE LITURGICAL CALENDAR

Another element of Christian liturgy derived from Judaism is the notion of the liturgical calendar. Jews celebrate four main feasts — Passover, Pentecost (Shevuoth), Yom Kippur, and Tabernacles (Succoth). Other holy days are also celebrated — New Year (Rosh Hashanah), Hanukkah, and Purim. Furthermore, the

continued on next page...

rabbis had developed a lectionary cycle for the synagogue. Its core consisted of readings from the Torah (the first five books of the Bible), plus readings from the Psalms and the prophets (Haftoroth).

Christians have imitated both elements. A liturgical year begins with Advent, flowing to Christmas, Epiphany, Lent, Eastertide, Pentecost, and Ordinary Time, plus a variety of feasts celebrating the events of salvation and the lives of the saints.

Also, a liturgical cycle existed early, with the core being the four Gospels as requisite, plus readings from the epistles and other New Testament books, the Psalms, and other books of the Old Testament. Just as the covenant sacrifice was preceded by reading the Ten Commandments and the laws, so is the liturgy of the Eucharist preceded by the liturgy of the word of God. This is meant to stir up faith to further believe the words of Jesus in the Eucharist.

Most clearly, faith, celebration, and sacrifice belong together in the Eucharist. They nourish one another and challenge one another. Let us celebrate the Eucharist in this Year of Faith as our paramount opportunity for continued growth in love of God and neighbor.

DISCUSS

1. Do you consider attending Mass on Sunday to be a duty or an act of love?
2. In what ways does your faith in Jesus express itself through your worship?
3. What new insight about the link between worship and faith have you received from the Scripture in this chapter?

PRACTICE

This week, at Sunday Mass, pay particular attention to the structure of the liturgy to see how the Liturgy of the Word helps carry us into our assent of faith through the reception of Holy Communion. Spend a few minutes after Mass thanking God for the gift of faith.

Session 6

FAITH AND THE
NEW EVANGELIZATION

"Intent on gathering the signs of the times in the present of history, faith commits every one of us to become a living sign of the presence of the Risen Lord in the world. What the world is in particular need of today is the credible witness of people enlightened in mind and heart by the word of the Lord, and capable of opening the hearts and minds of many to the desire for God and for true life, life without end."

— Pope Benedict XVI,
Porta Fidei (n. 15)

It's not enough in this Year of Faith to simply renew our own personal beliefs and share with like-minded people in our churches. Recent popes have emphasized the need to revitalize our faith in God and share it with others in our de-Christianized culture through a "New Evangelization." Pope Benedict XVI has affirmed the seriousness of the need by establishing the Pontifical Council for the New Evangelization. And he has called a Synod on New Evangelization at the opening of the Year of Faith. But the pope is not only inviting the bishops to reflect on evangelization; he is urging every Catholic to become a new evangelizer:

"Anyone who has discovered Christ must lead others to him. A great joy cannot be kept to oneself. It has to be passed on."
— Pope Benedict XVI,
World Youth Day (August 21, 2005)

It is the role and duty of each of us to respond to this call.

CONSIDER

Blessed John Paul II coined the term "New Evangelization." He recognized the need to re-evangelize traditionally Christian nations that have drifted away from the faith. One of the "new" elements was his expectation that laypeople would take a lead in advancing the Gospel since the mission fields for evangelization were no longer in faraway places. The pope charged us to share Christ and the Gospel even with people in our parishes, many of whom have been catechized and sacramentalized but have never been evangelized.

Thus, New Evangelization means calling everyone to have faith in God as he is revealed by Jesus Christ. It is a re-commitment to a personal love of Christ in union with the Church. It is a discovery of life and grace in the sacraments and a recovery of receiving the Bible as the word of God.

People of faith need to be aware of the new opportunities for this evangelization in the mass media, in the new media of the digital social networks, and through personal witness. Already, many Christians are making efforts — in groups, in Church-sanctioned ministries, and as individuals — to make known the Gospel of Jesus Christ. All that it requires is an authentic faith in God, an increase of knowledge of the faith, and a love for the people we evangelize.

The stakes are high — eternity in either heaven or hell. Nonetheless, the possibilities are tremendous, the adventure is exciting, and the prospects for successful re-evangelization are great.

STUDY

To become effective evangelizers, we must understand the factors that have caused some to lose faith in God and the Church, and which have diminished it in many others. The roots of this loss of faith are many:

- **Rationalism:** The rise of the Enlightenment Era in the eighteenth century did much to promote the idea of using reason without faith to uncover every mystery of the universe. Some rationalistic people fear that God is purely a simplistic way to accept life's unknown mysteries. They believe that science will eventually fathom all unknowns and create a technological paradise for everyone.

- **Politics:** Many of the political ideologies that have sprung up in the last three centuries have been detrimental to Christianity. Some have tried to subsume the Church into the state. Others are totalitarian, placing the state or nation ahead of God and the Church. They have had a deleterious effect on people's attachment to faith and religion. In America, people on either end of the political spectrum may be tempted to focus more on party loyalty than on a Christian critique of the political, cultural, and moral agenda of their own party. This, too, can be a distraction from the faith.

- **Materialism:** This ideology insists that only the material world exists and that spirituality has no impact on "real" life. Marxism is the most explicitly materialistic of these theories, but a practical materialism has also affected many free-market and socialist economies. As a result, many people consider economic success to be more important than moral integrity, holiness, or eternal life in heaven.

- **Doubts:** The atheist movement denies God's existence in favor of science, but its recent tactics have been to impugn

God's character rather than disprove his existence. Science cannot disprove God's existence, so prominent atheists such as Richard Dawkins make God, the Church, and Christians in general appear to be bad characters.

- **Neo-Gnosticism:** Writers such as Dan Brown, author of *The Da Vinci Code*, claim that the Church's rejection of Gnosticism was a political power play rather than a teaching of true Christianity. According to this way of thinking, Church dogmas and moral teaching merely manifest the Church's desire to control people's lives, and therefore all Church teaching is suspect.

- **Skepticism:** Some people simply do not want to be fooled by anyone — a good attitude to have. However, since some of these people know very little about the faith — and even less about its defense in history, science, and logic — they hold themselves aloof from making a faith commitment.

- **Immorality:** Some forms of immorality deaden the soul to the need for God — especially drugs, alcohol, sexual addiction, and other addictions. The conscience becomes suppressed until the pain of the sins begins to awaken the deep need for God. Other people take their sinful life as normal, and they do not want to change. They may even fear change and a moral improvement of life because they identify their ego with sinful behavior.

- **Loss:** Some people lose their faith in God because they have suffered a great loss. Since God did not answer their prayers in a dire situation the way they wanted, they reject God and choose not to believe.

CONSIDER

The new evangelizers must become sensitive to the varying spiritual conditions and needs of the people to whom they present the Gospel of Christ. Jesus and the apostles could safely assume faith in God and in the inspiration of the Old Testament during their public ministry; that is not always the case in the modern world. Therefore, we must know the people we are evangelizing. Listen to their stories, concerns, fears, angers, questions, doubts, and needs. Sensitivity to others is an important starting point for the New Evangelization. That is how we learn to scratch where the other person truly itches.

RESOURCES FOR EVANGELIZATION

 There are many wonderful resources for learning how to explain the faith — a theological science known as apologetics. Here are some of my favorites:

- *Radio Replies* (three volumes), by Father Leslie Rumble and Father Charles M. Carty (TAN Books, 1979)
- *Catholicism and Fundamentalism: The Attack on "Romanism" by "Bible Christians,"* by Karl Keating (Ignatius Press, 1988)
- *The Question Box,* by Rev. Bertrand L. Conway, C.S.P. (Paulist Press, 1929)
- *How to Defend the Faith without Raising Your Voice: Civil Responses to Catholic Hot Button Issues,* by Austen Ivereigh (Our Sunday Visitor, 2012)
- *The Church and New Media: Blogging Converts, Online Activists, and Bishops Who Tweet,* by Brandon Vogt (Our Sunday Visitor, 2011)
- *The Fathers Know Best: Your Essential Guide to the Teachings of the Early Church,* by Jimmy Akin (Catholic Answers, 2010)
- *Theology and Sanity,* by F. J. Sheed (Ignatius Press, 1993)
- Almost any book by C. S. Lewis or G. K. Chesterton.

The Year of Faith is a time of renewal and knowledge of our faith so that we can become better evangelizers. This time of rekindling and deepening can motivate us to search more deeply into our own questions and those of the people around us.

We should not fear the questions we cannot answer. Rather, let them motivate us to search out the issues more deeply and seek out sources that show us how to defend the faith in the modern world.

We can learn to put the faith into words. In language study, we speak of active and passive knowledge of a language. For instance, I can read articles in French; this is passive knowledge, by which I recognize what the words mean. However, I do not speak French — I have no active knowledge for putting thoughts into French sentences. Most Catholics recognize the teaching of the faith when they see it — passive knowledge — but many do not know how to explain it to someone else — active knowledge. The Year of Faith is a summons to acquire active knowledge so that every Catholic can participate in the New Evangelization.

CONSIDER

While the Year of Faith is meant to help us learn our faith better so we can evangelize better, we still need to remember that *faith* and *love* belong together. Love of the person we evangelize is an essential attitude and decision for the evangelizer. We do not preach just to win arguments with unbelievers. Neither do we evangelize to win more people to our side. We evangelize because we love.

This love has different dimensions. On the one hand, we care about the present situation of people. Their need for acceptance, for hope, for meaning, and for personal depth presses upon their life right now. People's loneliness, poverty, moral problems, and addictions are urgent concerns. We need to address these issues with a view to their best interests. We can let them know of the love of Jesus Christ, both in our words and actions, which we do for their sake, not ours.

On the other hand, we must also love them enough to be concerned for their eternal life. We want not only the present best for them but also the eternal best. We must remember that God loves them infinitely, and his desire to bring them to heaven is infinitely greater than even their own desire to share his eternal joy in heaven. As evangelists, we simply want to share in God's infinite love for the other person's eternal welfare.

We also need the Holy Spirit to empower us if we are to become evangelizers that are apt tools in God's hands. First, he will strengthen the inner person with his gifts: "The Spirit of the Lord shall rest upon him, the spirit of wisdom and understanding, the spirit of counsel and might, the spirit of knowledge and the fear of the Lord. And his delight shall be in the fear of the Lord" (Is 11:2-3). God will grant us holy boldness to step out and evangelize, even when our human nature makes us afraid to take that risk.

INVESTIGATE

FRUITS OF THE HOLY SPIRIT

 The Holy Spirit will temper our holy boldness to evangelize with his fruits: "The fruit of the Spirit is love, joy, peace, patience, kindness, goodness, faithfulness, gentleness, self-control" (Gal 5:22-23).

Reflect on each of the fruits of the Holy Spirit.

How may each one have an effect on the way I evangelize?

_____

_____

_____

Which of these fruits do I think I need the most in order to be effective in the New Evangelization?

_____

_____

_____

CONSIDER

God's grace is paramount in any evangelizing we may do. We remember that faith is a grace from God — that is why we call faith a theological virtue. As a mere human being, I am incapable of giving anyone the gift of faith. Neither can I save them. Only God grants faith and saves their immortal souls. All I can do is cooperate with God and let him act without my interference.

Part of my role in this process is to know faith and apologetics so that I can give the reasons to believe. But since God alone can offer someone the gift of saving faith, my other role is to pray, fast, and offer sacrifices so that the person may receive the gift of faith and salvation.

When someone resists our efforts, or rejects us and what we say, we must become all the more committed to prayer and sacrifice for that person. In that process, we will love the individual all the more; it is very difficult to be angry at someone, or to become dejected, when we are praying for that person. Furthermore, we will grow in faith and trust in God as we learn to depend on him during our prayers. Ultimately, God will respond to those prayers in ways that will surprise and amaze us. Again, remember that God wants the person saved infinitely more than we do.

PRAYER AND EVANGELIZATION

 Another part of our role in evangelizing is to maintain an active prayer life. Prayer itself is a gift of God's grace. Pray for the Holy Spirit to fill your prayer life. He will move us to cry out, "Abba! Father!" to God (Rom 8:15; Gal 4:6). He will stir our hearts to proclaim that "Jesus is Lord" (1 Cor 12:3). Let the Holy Spirit enrich our prayer life so that it is deep and nourishing to the soul. Meditative listening to God makes the truth of the faith increasingly an integral and integrating part of our life. That resonant truth will be apparent to others without our trying to make it apparent. Prayer will make God's truth our own truth.

INVESTIGATE

GIFTS OF THE HOLY SPIRIT

St. Paul lists the gifts of the Holy Spirit in three different letters.

Stop here and read **1 Corinthians 12-14**, **Romans 12:3-8**, and **Ephesians 4:4-16** in your own Bible.

Note the various gifts that St. Paul lists. How many gifts are mentioned in more than one list?

The New Evangelization will bring every believer who undertakes it into new adventures. Living the faith will become more than a comfort or source of life's meaning. The faith will become exciting beyond our expectations. Answer the call to evangelize anew so that faith can be revitalized — faith among the people of modern society and culture, as well as our own faith. Be open to letting the Holy Spirit give you great gifts to help your evangelization activity. Do not let fear hold you back, but let God's grace move you forward in this Year of Faith.

DISCUSS

1. How have you brought the message of the Gospel to others in your life?

2. What holds you back from living your faith in a way that makes others want to know more about it?

3. What new insight regarding sharing the faith have you received from Scripture in this chapter?

PRACTICE

This week, be bold enough to share your faith and love of the Lord with one person, trusting that the Holy Spirit will guide your words and actions.

AN ACT OF FAITH

O my God, I firmly believe that you are one God in three divine Persons, Father, Son, and Holy Spirit; I believe that your divine Son became man and died for our sins, and that he shall come to judge the living and the dead. I believe these and all the truths that the holy Catholic Church teaches, because you have revealed them, who can neither deceive nor be deceived.